EMERGING

Tara Hall

CONTENTS

Foreword

DR. ALISHA N. HILL

Tara's journey has transformed lives in person and throughout the pages of her books. Tara Hall is an authentic trailblazer, who is compassionate, yet graced with the understanding and drive to emerge impossibilities forward into possibilities.

"When you can become enchanted by who you are, when you can forgive the part of you that betrayed you, then you will be seen and heard and nothing less than captivating." Wokie Nwabueze (Founder of Women Prepared to Lead)

Such a powerful quote by a powerful emerging leading woman. This quote speaks as a bedrock for it lays the very foundation of what the visionary of EMERGING stands. Visionary author Tara Hall executed the vision and purpose that God gave her to collaborate with women of all ethnic groups, socio-economic backgrounds, various faith, and religious designations. Tara has succeeded out of life's triumphs and moments of jubilee, like becoming a Certified Jack Canfield Trainer and Coach, to opening the gates of confidence building at the Women Build Confidence Conference where we met in 2018. I have facilitated alongside and been a recipient of Tara's strategic coaching style. Tara has also emerged from the arena of pain. Tara fully understands what it takes to overcome fears, pains, anxieties, in order to emerge into purpose and stability. As an emerging woman, my passion is to connect with women who find themselves at crossroads in life. Women wanting to leave the yesterday of defeat and emerge into the woman of tomorrow. Tara has been a pivotal part of my acceleration to emerging into my destiny. Tara is a sister-friend, a coach, a mentor and an emerging leader to many. Her gift to bring such a collaborative work together is impeccable. This book unveils the stories of truth, resilience and emerging out of hard spaces and places as told by women just like you and me.

EMERGING, is a book for every woman, from every race, every space, rags to riches, from coast to coast. You will find healing for your soul, water for your dry places, encouragement for our low space, beauty of the ashes of your past. Turn the pages slow and take each journey, as you arrive at a destination of revealing truths. You too will see the EMERGING of a new and improved YOU!

Founder & CEO
DrHillSpeaks
HealHerCircles
A.L.I.V.E

Acknowledgement

I want to thank God for allowing me to Emerge into this next chapter of life. He has divinely placed the right people, places and things in my path to birth this vision of women coming together for a greater good. I also thank my international Jumpstart to Success Facebook community who help to serve as ongoing inspiration on the journey. I am grateful to the eleven brave women of Emerging for fearlessly stepping out of their comfort zones to benefit that young girl or grown woman who may be blocked by fear or a storm in her life. These eleven women made a bold decision to live out loud by inviting us into their hearts and minds with empowering messages.

A special thank you to my Emerging business women who continue to show up authentically and courageously:

Jessica Bahtuoh, Realtor Pro Flat Fee Realty on fb Jess Bahtuoh
Carol Balbuena, "The Spanish Insurance Lady" on IG@callcarolb
Maggie Ngere, crushthatdebtnow.com
Allysia Richardson, arideafactory.com
Danielle Scott, Danielle-Scott.com

Visionary Author, Tara Hall

WHY WE MUST EMERGE

So, what does it really mean to Emerge? It can mean to come out of, step into, grow, or develop. As I apply Emerging to my life, it's an evolution of growth. It's the freedom that I have fully embraced and have tapped into unapologetically.

We all have different seasons in our lives and as with each new season, we evolve and shed old thoughts, behaviors and actions. We become anew with our own vibrant colors and clear paths. We give ourselves permission to rebuild and trust our inner compass, only then can we accept ALL of who we are to forge into our next.

On my personal evolution of growth, I learned to trust and believe in me. As referenced in my first publication, The Power of 5%: Success Lessons to Amplify Your Life, I remark "success is an inside job." When we learn to let go of old chapters, stained thoughts and beliefs, we start to collect new evidence of who we can become.

Private victories in life are more celebrated when you can freely accept the flaws, defects and prior misgivings when you accept that those too are part your evolution. Unlike animals, human beings have unlimited potential. How unfair to those around us to not utilize every ounce of it while we are still given the gift of breath!

"Not used up" is a phrase often used by Les Brown in his reference to what we do not want written on our tombstones. We owe it to ourselves and others to ensure we use our gifts, passions, and skills to the utmost while here on earth.

As I emerged from despair and situational depression after the loss of my first child, I found myself living but not fully engaged in life for a period of time in 2002. I later learned the difference between being alive and living. It wasn't until I gained the tools to release the guilt and shame of that experience that I was able to emerge from that season of my life. What are you coming out of? What are you heading towards? Do you trust you again? Do you forgive you? Get quiet and reflect on ways you can EMERGE too!

Making a conscious commitment to stay in personal development is my choice. Just as I have made other choices, this one is different.

This one feels aligned with who I knew I could be from the time I was in my 20's. Remember, everything comes in its due time! Everyone's journey will not look or feel the same, otherwise it isn't unique to YOU. What I do know, however is that the journey can be as sweet as you want it to be. You just have to make a choice.

This compilation of Emerging is the next step in applying the method of five percent more in the H.O.W.(helping other women). In the next several pages, you have the privilege of stepping into the minds and hearts of eleven beautiful women who share what Emerging has looked like in their lives. Each story is unique just like yours. You will find a story that may resonate with an experience in your life. You will also gain a tool to step into or out of a particular season of your life. Just know, you are not alone. You can rebuild, restore and replenish your reservoir with support.

As long as you have the breath of life, YOU are "not used up." Get back in the game of life and step into your next chapter to EMERGE!

About the Author

Tara Hall is an amazon international best-selling author and visionary of the Emerging compilation. As the owner of Tara Hall Inspired Solutions LLC, a personal and professional training and development company, she offers customized trainings in person or virtually in leadership, communication skills, and confidence coaching. She has over 20 years of combined experience in leadership, career coaching and training. She is a Certified Jack Canfield Trainer in the Success Principles, Inspirational Speaker, and Facilitator. She was recognized as a 2020 Woman Rising Honoree by the Connecticut Women's Business Development Council. She holds a Bachelor of Arts Degree in Communications and a Master of Science Degree in Organizational Management. She has two pending co-author publications to be released in 2021. It's her mission to help others reclaim their lives by exercising their voices and sharing their gifts.

The Gift Within

ERICA CASTILLO

I am reminded of the scripture that says, "Do not neglect the gift that is in you." 1 Timothy 4:14. Yet we do this all too often. Why do we do this…...? One reason, FEAR.

Your gift

"Everyone has a gift, but not every person recognizes what his or her gift is. Being able to identify it is the key to fulfilling the unique purpose of your life."

— Steve Harvey

You see, we all possess a gift that is in us. A gift that is given to us by our Creator. You have a gift that needs to be opened, used, and shared. Pablo Picasso, says "The meaning of life is to find your gift, the purpose of life is to give it away." What's your gift, you may be wondering?

What is it that you are passionate about?....Ah. There lies your gift, your purpose. You see your gift is that thing that you are so passionate about, it just overwhelms your heart. It's near and dear to your heart. It's that one thing you love that brings joy. When you operate in your gift, it brings you purpose and fulfillment. It's what you were born to do and it comes naturally. Look at what other people appreciate and admire about you. Listen to the words that they use to describe you. Your gift lies there!

Take a moment to sit and reflect. Is it singing, dancing, playing a musical instrument or writing music? Do you have a way with words, language, telling stories? Is it cooking, designing, building? Perhaps its speaking, teaching, coaching, or organizing. We have all been given unique abilities and talents.

As I think back from childhood to adulthood, I have always been that person, who wants to help someone in need or willing to share or give up what I have to meet their need. Or share information or knowledge to improve their situation. I am the "problem-solver." A person who questions what's unjust and stands up for what's right is what brings me joy. My love for helping others live a better life led me to a helping profession, as a social worker. My commitment is to advocacy, social justice, helping individuals, families, and communities. As social workers, we care about people, we want to make things better, to bring relief to the grieved and distressed. Above all, we want our work to make a difference.

Assisting and serving others has been a common thread throughout my life. Shared thoughts from family, friends, peers, professional colleagues, and associates often told me that I can be inspirational, compassionate, knowledgeable, and a critical thinker. Yet, I could not fully recognize these talents in me. For years, I often wondered what was my gift and life purpose. It was not until recently, that I came to recognize that my gift is educating, inspiring, and serving others.

Your Gift Wrapped in Fear

"The fears we don't face become our limits."

— Robin Sharma

Fear is a natural, powerful, and primitive human emotion. The power of it can stop us in our tracks, prevent us from reaching our full potential, and living out our life purpose. So many of us have unused gifts that are wrapped in fear. Do you have unused gifts?

Our gifts may be wrapped in the fear of judgement and rejection. We fear that people may not accept or receive our gift. You may think what you have to offer is not good enough. Or our past insecurities may cause us to feel less than. Then, we have those gifts that are wrapped in the fear of failure. We are often held back by the limiting thoughts of actually achieving the success that we hope for!

The fear of judgment, rejection, and failure all kept me silent and a hostage to sharing my gifts. As a woman, a black woman at that, I felt an enormous pressure to succeed and achieve. Although I am well educated with a Master of Social Work Degree with a concentration in Community Administrative Practice, years of worked, and lived experience, I still at times find myself feeling incapable, unqualified, and unworthy. Frustrated by my inner critic and conversations, of Am I good enough? Will people accept me? Am I eloquent enough? Do I need more degrees? And the list could go on and on. One day I simply asked myself, "Am I more powerful than my fear?"

Unwrap Your Gift

"Don't let fear stop you. Don't give up because you are paralyzed by insecurity or overwhelmed by the odds, because in giving up, you give up hope. Understand that failure is a process in life, that only in trying can you enrich yourself and have the possibility of moving forward. The greatest obstacle in life is fear and giving up because of it."

— Sonia Sotomayor

It is due time to unwrap those gifts, someone is waiting to be emerged and liberated because you made a choice! Push past where you would normally stop, and challenge your doubts and beliefs. Is what you think about yourself, really true? Cancel out the inner critic and replace it with affirmations. Your gifts matter and have value. "You have not lived today until you have done something for someone who can never repay you." — Jon Bunyan.

I choose to move beyond the fear of judgement, rejection. and failure. I choose to use my talents without being worried about my flaws or imperfections. I am emerging from a place of FEAR to FAITH. Being true to the calling on my life, trusting and being a good steward of the gifts that were given to me. "I am careful not to confuse excellence with perfection. Excellence I can reach for; perfection is God's business." - Michael J. Fox

Share your gift

"Your talent is God's gift to you. What you do with it is your gift back to God."

— Leo Buscaglia

To share your gifts is to be a good steward of what God has given you. We have a responsibility to develop, cultivate, and refine our talents. Sharing with others provides an opportunity for them to learn and grow. In return, you bring hope and change!

I now know my gifts. It has taken me a long time to feel secure and confident to STATE THAT- to WALK IN IT with no apologies. My gifts serve as inspiration, motivation, empowerment, and encouragement for others. My hope is to inspire others to live their passion. I have a burning desire and drive to make a positive impact in individuals and my community. It starts by writing, being a part of this beautiful anthology, being among amazing women who are encouraging others to emerge to the next level, whether that be in their spiritual, personal, or professional journey. I continue to stay the course in my efforts of pursuing a career in social work academia and entrepreneurship. The opportunity to mentor, teach, and educate with the goal to make a long-term impact on students' lives. I am playing a part in closing the racial wealth gap by becoming a black female business owner by building generational wealth, supporting a cause, and uplifting my community. Moving forward in my steps to start a non-profit organization that will benefit children and families, I will give back to what the community gave me. Using the gift within.

"When I stand before God at the end of my life, I would hope that I would not have a single bit of talent left, and could say, 'I used everything You gave me."

— Chadwick Aaron Boseman

About the Author

Erica Rena Castillo has 14 plus years of social work experience. Mrs. Castillo was a former Social Worker with the State of Connecticut, Department of Child and Families for 10 years. She received her Master of Social Work degree with a concentration in Community and Administrative Practice at the University of Texas Arlington. Mrs. Castillo is a member with the National Association of Social Work, NASW. She serves as the Communications Committee Chair for NASW Texas—Fort Worth Area Branch.

Mrs. Castillo currently enjoys her position, as a program director for Challenge of Tarrant County. Mrs. Castillo is also pursuing other career endeavors that includes becoming an author, professor, social work entrepreneur, and starting a non-profit organization. And most importantly, she is devoted to her supportive husband, Jose Castillo of 19 years with two amazing children, Ebony and Brian. Mrs. Castillo hopes to leave a legacy for her children of the importance of education, entrepreneurship, and public service. Connect on LinkedIn, Facebook@Erica Castillo-Carroll or Instagram@ericacastillocarroll

Hearing Voices

ROWANA GRADY

Looking up at the ceiling almost close enough to touch from the bunk, I was more passive than I'd been in ages; 14, 15, years old and I lost count. I laid there feeling my heartbeat in the hollow of my torso. I was as restful as a child in the arms of momma and an outlaw needing a washing from the water of God at the same time. My eyes surveyed the room capturing images of the lifers. I feared no evil! I really didn't care to move about, in fact, going to the restroom was like walking through the valley of the shadow of death row. Fortunately, it was only a shadow. Never had it dawned on me that bravery must be exercised with caution. One glance in the mirror beheld a faded flower displaced from an orchid, refusing to die like the fallen leaves of autumn do. Gazing relentlessly in the shadowy glass was like staring into the eyes of a lioness underestimated by hyenas laughing at the lack of victory. Holding the oversized nightgown up from the floor, I made my way back to the upper bunk.

After running away, like Ann Darrow, knowing King Kong would stop at nothing until he had her in his hand, running from God was exhausting. I just laid there flirting with my childhood. I pictured momma singing in the choir as my sister and I watched the tears roll down her face as she vocalized loving Him. I was too young to conceptualize her tears. Neither did I understand suddenly leaving Tacoma after dad's mental breakdown on Fort Lewis. Momma got really quiet, hardly ever left the house. The silence of her depression screamed. The guard finally turned the lights out.

As the nights grew into the darkest hours, I'd bring heartbreaks to the picture window of my mind. I wondered why I stayed when my boyfriend's lack of commitment spoke volumes. But how could he walk away with a friend? She was family. What a difficult disrespect. Working through the humiliation was a full-time position. The butterflies in my stomach entertained forgiving them, but forgiveness was buried deep down in my underdeveloped parts of my being. I was dressed to kill. I had to take off resentment, frustration, and anger; I bore the naked pain. For the first time I understood "The heart is deceitful above all things, and desperately wicked, who can know it" (Jeremiah 17:9). The Good Book taunted me, echoing, "God examines the heart." I certainly knew He could see in the darkest places.

Packing to go home was interesting because I didn't have one. I reflected deeply. Let it go was the theme of every thought. On that day, I heard, "court run." I came down from the bunk ready to ride the bus back to God knows where. My feelings were ambiguous, but I was set on roughing it out. I went far away to start from nowhere. Feeling like Jada when she got away in the movie, Set it Off, I knew I could never go back. It was bittersweet though, knowing I couldn't retrieve the pictures of my mom and recover other sentimental items from the boarded up apartment. Dozing off on the bus, I wondered what happened to Andre; I'll never forget sitting on the hallway steps with him, hustling, when I began singing, What Shall I Render. He looked at me and passionately said, "you don't belong here." The essence of his words remains potent.

Every now and again I'd get a lump in my throat, smothering grief. This is the one-year anniversary of mamma's death, I whispered. Struggling not to hate her offender; I wondered how they met. I can still hear grandpa saying, *"Run him away from there!"*, but we turned a blind eye because mom was smiling again. Like a pressure cooker, I'd let the agony out a little at a time. Understanding the predisposition of mental illness, my mind, I knew I had to fight for it. But I remembered a little recipe, that "if I wait on the Lord, He will renew my strength; I'll mount up with wings like an eagle, run and not be weary, walk and not faint" (Isaiah 40:31). So, I just waited on the Lord.

Standing on the balcony of the homeless shelter smoking and enjoying the cool of early November, out of nowhere I heard a whisper, "God breathed the breath of life into Adam." Startled, I immediately tossed it overboard. Reflecting on the times grandma would say God spoke to her; I finally understood. After all that running, the Lord was still right there. I heard it once, but it played in my head a thousand times. I never smoked again.

I stood freezing at the bus stop 7:30 in the morning, trying to figure things out. I thought it would be nice if they allowed us to stay in until nine when more facilities were open. I walked in the room feeling like a fish out of water. I finally said, *"I'm looking for Ms. Brown."* A petite little White lady looked up over her glasses while working with another student. Our eyes met in an awkward silence; I never said a word. She worked her way over to me and asked, "What's your highest level of education?" I softly said ninth. Scanning the test booklet, I picked up the pencil. Walking to her desk holding the fully completed booklet, Ms. Brown worriedly stared at me. "Oh, you're done?" I nodded and left the class. I heard her from the hallway, "come back in 15 minutes please." Afterwards, she came over to me with a grimace on her face saying, "you're ready, go register."

Ms. Brown pleaded for my return in the interim of the scheduled exam. She was a little quirky, but sincere. I liked her; she didn't need to be told Black lives matter. She would call early, seeming somewhere between sorry to bother you and I'm not taking no for an answer. I was quiet, but clearly rough around the edges. "I just want to make sure you're coming to campus today" she'd say. It felt like I was doing it for her, and I wouldn't dare let her down. I took the exam and Ms. Brown's nerves were a wreck! Calling the test offices and asking around, she finally got answers. "You passed! You passed!" she said excitedly. I was still cocooning between lifestyles. "Come down for a scholarship opportunity to do whatever you want" and the money was right on time. Ms. Brown still kept her foot in the door; "let me introduce you to some professors" she pleaded. Showcasing my Master's degree in the curio of my limited valuables remains a conversation piece about Ms. Brown.

Sitting in the quiet of my home caring for my newborn god baby, a Program Director called. "Hey, I'm so glad you still have this number; we have an opening I think you'd be great for." I attended their support group several years prior. At the time, I was working in a beauty parlor where I was enthralled by a man who could spot a sapiosexual anywhere. He was a beautiful stud and very calculated. It was like being in full moon with a vampire, bitten, and yoked to his testosterone. Running back to the altar of God was at Olympic speed. Nevertheless, I never knew the Program Director envisioned me as a colleague. I went in for the interview and bumped into the friend who previously walked away with my love. She was living in one of the houses I would govern if selected for the position. The pain was long gone. I still wondered if she would sabotage my opportunity. Either way, she was forgiven.

While being employed in criminal/restorative justice, I moved around within the organization working with men and women and catering to a plethora of their needs. They commonly had childhood trauma, and I wanted to understand that. I had an unfavorable background, but I let God be God. While sitting in a training, a woman came up whispering, "I couldn't part with your application." She remembered my name. I smiled knowing "The king's heart is in the hand of the Lord [and] he turns it wherever he wants" (Proverbs 21:1).

New to the office, I overheard a worker say, "they're getting rid of her." Interestingly enough, I had to keep encouraging myself. I would inwardly tell myself "hold your head up." One day Kevin walked over asking nonchalantly, "So, they're letting you go?" I was certain I was an office rumor. Though I oftentimes humored myself, it was challenging seeing the red carpet roll out for the other new people. While walking to the parking lot, I heard a whisper, "no man can close". I sat in the car googling the terms and found this, "I know your works. I have set before you an open door, and no one can shut it" (Rev 3:8a). I knew then that the King of authority was deciding my plateau. The perks of knowing the Lord were mounting. So, there I sat, year after year, listening intently at the Relationships Matter Conferences, with rivers of gratitude flowing in my soul.

Sitting in my home office reading the reference letters that supported my pardon, I was taken for a walk down memory lane. I wasn't really one for skeletons but worrying about who was gonna carry a bone was daunting. Despite the good, bad, beautiful, and the ugly, God was a whole vibe. Turning on YouTube, listening to Leandria sing "He Was There All the Time", I testify that "the favor of the Lord is for a lifetime" (Psalms 30:5). My most precious takeaway in everything that I've endured is discovering that "The foundation of God stands sure, having this seal, The Lord knows them that are His" (2 Tim 2:19). If you ever wonder why I get quiet at times, I'm probably just listening.

Many children grow up in chaotic environments, often leading to experimental and unguided behaviors that can evolve into young adulthood. Oftentimes, we take on professions to participate in the nation's health. It is necessary to assess at times if we believe in the work we do. When individuals defy the status quo, why do we struggle to offer them a seat at the table? We sometimes fail to reject our embedded hypotheses deeming people unintelligible, incapable or undeserving. Implicit bias shows up and can operate as a sniper if we are not constantly sorting through our snapshot judgements. Finally, we oftentimes marginalize what religion is to a person. We don't like to validate religion and spirituality as a meaningful part of healing, resilience, and success. What's our next move when a person's narrative doesn't imitate mainstream ideals? That is the question. My ultimate hope is that this read will re-inspire us to intentionally make a difference.

About the Author

Rowana Grady is from Tacoma Washington and spent most of her life in Connecticut. She is currently in her final year as a doctoral candidate in Professional Leadership from Northcentral University. Her dissertation focus is understanding religion in social work practice. She earned a Bachelor Degree in Urban Studies and a Master of Social Work Degree from the University of Connecticut. Rowana is currently employed as a child protection services worker with a strong background in restorative justice. She was featured in JDPP's In My Shoes performance project and was later granted a record expungement from the CT Department of Pardons and Parole. She is active in her church community and applies scripture to her everyday living. Rowana professes that Jesus is the best thing she ever paid attention to. This author is known for her kindness and is easy to talk to. She carries a burden for trafficked children and hopes to eventually educate social workers on understanding religion and spirituality in practice.

Approaching Freedom

RENEE HOFF

My personal story will take you on a journey of interpersonal reflections and revelations as I move toward freedom. According to Merriam-Webster, freedom as a noun is the power of the right to act, speak or think as one wants without hindrance or restraint. While freedom has a broad range of application, it applies to me internally since childhood. Having grown up during the turbulent 60's presented many challenges and opportunities for African Americans. The racial tension that gripped the United States resulted in some of the most crucial periods of the Civil Rights Movement. As an African American, this was a defining moment in history.

My parents were cognizant of the changes that were unfolding as a result of the Civil Rights Movement and prepared me to adapt to many of the situations they had not even experienced as the country transitioned from segregation to integration. My early childhood education began with being the first person in my immediate family to attend an integrated school. It was a frightening time in my life. Under normal circumstances, transitioning from home to school creates anxiety, but breaking racial barriers added another level of fear. It soon became apparent that my parents would not always be present to support me when dealing with or being confronted with situations from peers at school. Imagine growing up being compared to the fictional character Olive Oyl from the popular TV 60's animated cartoon Popeye! This was a frequent occurrence with other students at school, on the playground, passing through the hallways or even in the community. Olive Oyl was a coy flapper who was tall, with a very thin build and enormous feet.

It was coincidental that the cartoon character and my statue had many similarities. It is amazing how childhood experiences can impact one's mindset. Being compared to Olive Oyl, started my journey to self-doubt and low self-esteem which caused me to become self-conscious about my physical appearance for many years to come. At a very early age, my height soared to 5'9' in middle school. Being very thin, usually referred to as skinny, with large feet, wearing size 10 shoes, glasses and having a gap in my teeth, gave peers a lot of ammunition to tease and bully me. Often times, I made efforts to camouflage what I perceived to be flawed characteristics. This was a full-time job during my formative years. Although my family provided generous positive praise, it never overshadowed the sneers and cheers from the bullies. The insults and jokes pierced deeply in my soul and over time created low self-esteem which slowly eroded my childhood, carefree spirit. Sadly, at that time, I secretly wanted to look like the "white girls" in hopes I would then be accepted. Only after becoming a young adult, I realized that being tall, slim, and having unique features were the perfect combination and ingredients that most models cherished. If I could only have loved then, the skin I was in!

During my early years, my family resided in newly integrated communities with racial tension resulting in my feeling isolated. I was already struggling to fit in and now loneliness was added to the list of my pain. There were no opportunities for me to hang out with my peers. To top it off, we moved to a suburban residential area becoming the only family of color. Most of the children attended private schools in the neighborhood while others were bused to an inner-city school. As you can imagine, it was a challenge for me to be bused to an unfamiliar community. For me, those bus rides were filled with anything but laughter and giggling with the other little girls.

As the years progressed, my self-image sank lower and lower as I tried to develop new relationships with my peers. I had an idea, "What if I started competing with them through sports?" "Then, I'd be accepted and part of the team." Sadly, this didn't work and the energy I exerted to keep this up dwindled quickly. Rather than embracing my talents and skills, my efforts then focused on seeking the approval of others. Something that would follow me later in life.

As high school approached, not being with my culture daily and having to adjust with the majority created an environment of not being accepted in either world! Not being urban enough by some kids and too urban for the families in my neighborhood was confusing and EXHAUSTING! My high school was tough, a true culture shock but yet the familiar discomfort of being an outsider remained present. There was a vast difference between being raised in the suburbs and being raised in the urban community. I continued to mask my inner pains of rejection while the voices of others continued to drown my spirit and ability to hear my own voice. My silenced voice showed up as the "people pleaser."

Moving towards adulthood and reflecting on my journey, I became aware of the experiences and patterns that lead to my lack of confidence. Despite all my positive attributes of being college educated, having a great sense of humor, gregariousness and attractiveness, I knew I had to do my internal work if I were to live my best life.

My first realization was that I am a child of God, born and equipped with everything to fulfill my purpose in life. This revelation was the beginning of becoming free to be me. Now, I cleanse myself of the toxic patterns that created a disregard for my self-worth. The notion that someone did not understand, love or appreciate me is no longer an issue for me to solve alone. In fact, it isn't even my business. Dismissing the labels of "people pleaser" or "enabler" has given me permission to be free. I now take personal responsibility and accountability for my behavior, choices and actions. I accept the outcome of my own doing and no longer blame others for what happens in my life. The poem "Invictus" by Victorian Era English poet William Ernest Henley (1849–1903) says it best in his last two lines "I am the master of my fate: I am the captain of my soul."

Have you ever had someone say "You are too nice?" "You always put people ahead of you?" It's as if your core qualities are something to be ashamed of. This was me and it was part of my DNA striving to be kind and giving. However, others often took this as my weakness. It was natural for me to do for others even if it was something I didn't want to do. I was uncomfortable exercising my "no." I realized I was not acting as the master of my fate at that time nor was I the captain of my soul either.

Once foggy, I now have a clear picture of what created failed relationships, complicated communications and other conflicts. Vowing to do things differently in my future is part of my true transformation. The bible says in Romans 12:2, "Do not be conformed to this world, but be transformed by the renewal of your mind, that by testing you may discern what is the will of God, what is good and acceptable and perfect." My goal is to fulfill my God given purpose rather than prioritizing the wishes of others over mine.

Every experience I've had has been a learning opportunity. Even lessons learned from my marriage that ended in divorce provided growth, a greater sense of understanding and better communication with others. Relationships with my family and friends is easier for me because I am no longer compelled to live out of my "stinkin' thinkin'" any longer. My voice is no longer silenced and I am loving the skin I am in!

As a parent, my children benefitted from my newly learned lessons by being more self-assured and confident in their own skin. When I realized my daughter was experiencing some of the same behavior from her peers, I was equipped with new tools, language and action to help her realize her worth. On the other hand, my son always turned a deaf ear to criticism, a lesson that could have served me well back then! While we did not have a perfect life, we experienced a wholesome, and healthy family environment grounded within a spiritual and supportive system. The days of allowing myself to agonize over an unwanted divorce, allowing dreams to die, overeating, becoming bitter, and looking into the mirror seeing someone unrecognizable faded just like a sunset.

My transformational journey began with a new mindset taking me from unresolved to reconciled. My future was about to shine bright! The childlike voice that was drowned out by the sounds of other's opinions had been replaced with a woman's voice who was embracing all she knew she could be. This woman is poised and positioned with self-love and acceptance. I am liberated from the debilitating self-doubt. I "fit in" just fine in my new skin layered in joy and happiness. No longer would the old wounds or negative inner chatter take stage. My family and friends would see the new me front and center like the lead actor in a play.

I have a new appreciation for others, and they have a new appreciation for me. As I turn the curve towards my 60's, my inner souls work continues to develop on a deeper level. Transformation is not easy but necessary if you are serious about becoming free. Self-examination is good for the soul. It's an opportunity to refresh, restore and reflect. Do you make time to do this? What have you learned?

I challenge all that read this chapter to revisit old thoughts and beliefs you may have accepted in the past. Replace those with daily positive mantras and affirmations. You will then find yourself on the road to freedom. Changing one's mindset changes one's life. Practicing positive behaviors and habits yield positive outcomes. We all deserve to be the best we can be. A close friend once told me to accept all my imperfections, limits, flaws, bad habits, weaknesses and to forgive myself for ever thinking I was not worthy. He was right! "I had to forgive me first." I didn't know what I didn't know and now I know better, so I'll continue to do better.

I am becoming the person God intended me to be and being on the right path reinforces that God has a plan for each of us. My journey is liberating, as I approach my freedom, which is guided by my new inner spirit and voice that says, "I am the master of my fate: I am the captain of my soul". I am approaching Freedom.

About the Author

Renee Hoff, LMSW is a regional manager for the State of Connecticut where she has been employed for over 30 years. She is also a part-time clinician at Southern Behavior Health. Ms. Hoff is the mother of two adult children, Janelle and Kevin. She is grandmother to Easton, Kayci, Chayce and Karter. As a proud member of Alpha Kappa Alpha Sorority Incorporated, she dedicates this chapter to all women who have achieved and are searching for freedom! Connect with Renee on LinkedIn.

Grace Is My Story

TINA JEFFERSON

"I have learned that success is to be measured not so much by the position that one has reached in life as by the obstacles which he has overcome while trying to succeed."

— Booker T. Washington

I am successful. Do you want to know why?...because I define success as happiness!

What makes me happy? My family, traveling, a clean house, a good book, a nice meal and a good movie. That order may change depending on the day!

During childhood, I was always surrounded by strong women. I've been fortunate to have fathers, uncles, brothers, nephews and sons…and I'm thankful for them all. However, growing up, women were the matriarchs of the family and they made a house a HOME. I always wanted a HOME. I've always loved the "traditional" family unit. I wanted to put a meal on the table for my family. A house, a husband, two kids and a dog. The traditional American family always represented happiness and adulthood for me. My favorite commercial growing up was a jingle "I can bring home the bacon, fry it up in a pan, and never let you forget you're a man…" However, my mother, and all the strong women in my family, taught me the importance of loving but not depending on a man. I was taught to put God first, value myself, value an education, to be independent and be able to take care of myself.

From a young age, there has always been a spiritual influence over my life. I come from a praying family. A proud African-American family with roots in the south. I was raised hearing about my great-grandfather being a preacher in Alabama. My mother told me stories about the Masons and Eastern Stars, and how my great-grandfather worked and my great-grandmother took care of the entire family. I was raised going to church with my mother, my godmother, and my aunt and uncle. My mother and godmother were Baptist, but my aunt and uncle were Pentecostal. Religiously, I associated more with the Baptist faith, but the Pentecostal church was more fun! My sisters, cousins and I liked to laugh at people "catching the holy ghost" and imitating them for entertainment after church.

We have all the same problems as any other family, but we love each other no matter what. Where I come from, you never "disown" your family. Family is never only people you are blood related to, it is always who you love and who loves you. It is normal in my family to have cousins raised like siblings, and to have grandparents take care of grandchildren. I have aunts, uncles, brother, sisters, cousins, some blood related and some not. Blood relation never has and never will be the ties that bind.

As an adult, I always had a plan. I set goals, worked hard, but I never strived for career and educational success at the cost of my family. Instead everything I did, I did for my FAMILY. I chose a career in social work because all children deserve a family and I wanted to support and strengthen families. When I first became a Mom, I sought a supervisory position so I could be home sooner with my daughter. I finished my Master of Social Work degree to obtain a higher position with better pay so I could do more for my family. I love vacations, making my family smile, and I love being able to provide a decent life for my children. I teach my children that education is important and to pick a career that is meaningful and will allow them to live the life they want. I also teach them to never put a career before happiness...family, travel, friends, and experiences, because it is the journey that matters. My mother always reminds me that your job will not surround your bed when your journey comes to an end. It will be your FAMILY.

So, when I was around 38 years old, I had accomplished all my goals. I was married with 2 children (a daughter and son), a house, 2 cars, a dog and career. My life was on schedule according to MY plan. On a beautiful day in April my husband, kids, and I had just returned from a business trip they had accompanied me on in Newport, Rhode Island. It was my first day back in the office so I expected work to be a little stressful. Working for a child protective services agency, you learn to expect the unexpected. However, this day was a little different. My co-worker and friend entered my office and shut the door. She told me she had something important and private to discuss with me. I had no idea that what she ended up saying would change my life forever, both personally and professionally.

She told me that my husband's 3 month old great nephew was placed into foster care the day before and needed a home. I sat there perplexed for a moment trying to take it all in. I asked "what happened?" along with all the why, when, and how questions you could imagine! It didn't dawn on me initially why she was really telling me. I thought it was because we had to plan for confidentiality because I was related. After answering all my questions, she kept standing there. Finally, she said, "Tina will you take him?"

I had never thought about more children. I had two C-sections and a tubal ligation right after the delivery of my son. I was content with the children God had blessed me. I had also vowed NEVER to take my work home. I prided myself in separating my personal and professional life. Even while working in the same city that I was born and raised, I thought I had to keep things compartmentalized in order to survive. However, for some unknown reason at that time, I found my next actions completely out of character for me. I called my husband, told him what was happening and asked him if we could take the baby. He held the phone silently for a few minutes processing all that I had said and his response could be summed up in two words, "You sure?" I didn't really have time to answer and what felt like a few minutes later, the cutest little chubby, curly haired baby boy in a powered blue sweat suit was brought into my office and placed in my arms. He smelled like the foster home he had just left, which I pictured to be an old woman who smoked cigarettes and cooked pork. He did not cry at all and snuggled into me with no hesitation. Over the next few hours, I was meeting a social worker at my home, talking to our children, buying a crib and baby formula and instantly becoming mother of three. I was initially happy and excited and soon thereafter extremely overwhelmed.

As a mom of two, I didn't appreciate the 10 months of pregnancy. The doctor's say it is 9 months...but it is actually 10! I enjoyed the first few months and hated the last. Not just because I was uncomfortable, but because I was inpatient. I wanted to know what my babies would look like, I wanted to hold them. The waiting period gives you time to plan, think, and decorate. What normally takes 10 months, occurred in 4 hours with my third child. After a few nights of the baby crying, which my husband mostly took care of, I was finally ready to answer his question from a few days earlier. Are you sure? No, no I wasn't sure at all. I admitted to myself that I wasn't ready to be a mom of an infant again. My entire life plan changed in real time. At 38 years old, I was parenting a newborn! I knew enough about child protective services to understand that the likelihood of my son going back to his biological mom was less than 50% on a good day. My plan of an empty nest had just taken a 6 year hit! See, what you don't understand from my story about my childhood, is I was the baby. My family had always raised me to understand that it takes a village to raise a child...BUT I was the baby! As the baby, I did what I wanted. I benefitted from all that my family provided, I got out of housework, trouble, and I even had lots of help raising my two children because I was the baby. I wasn't the one who had to sacrifice for others unless I chose to. My husband was an oldest child so birth order worked well in our relationship. He was accustomed to taking responsibility for others and I was accustomed to benefiting from everyone else's sacrifices. I was in a good position for 38 years.

Fortunately, my third child forced me to grow up in ways that I never imagined. He challenged my entire identity and how I defined a perfect family. I couldn't compartmentalize my life anymore. The personal and the professional had just collided in the messiest but yet most beautiful of ways. For 3 long years, different social workers were in and out of my home until the adoption was finalized.

Acknowledging my prior selfishness of my view as a wife, mother, and social worker, I realized now what it truly meant to "put God first" and become the "matriarch" of my new "traditional family."

One day, on the drive home from work, I tuned into a religious station giving a sermon about adoption. Because of my internal struggles, I listened intently and I wasn't disappointed. The preacher said sometimes God will bring people in your life not because you need them, but because they need YOU. The support of my family and hearing that sermon, helped change my perspective. It taught me to stop focusing on myself and what I wanted and instead to focus on what I could mean in the lives of others. My favorite quote by Forest E. Witcraft is "A hundred years from now it will not matter what my bank account was, the sort of house I lived in, or the kind of car I drove...but the world may be different because I was important in the life of a child."

How do you want to be remembered? What impact do you want to have on those that you love? What impact do you want to make on your job? What impact do you want to make on the world around you? In the play Hamilton, they ask, "Who will live to tell your story?" I reflected on the same questions. I aspire to be like all the strong women in my family who sacrificed for me and influenced my life. I want to be a blessing to the children's lives that I touch.

Emerging is a never ending journey until God calls you home. Emerging is about being the best version of yourself. Life, Love,

Happiness, and creating memories. It's learning how to GROW through changes knowing the sun will always shine in the morning. Emerging is realizing it is not about your plan, it's about GOD's plan for your life.

About the Author

Tina L. Jefferson, LMSW is abundantly blessed and highly favored. She is a wife, mother of three, daughter, sister, aunt and cousin. She is a graduate of the University of Connecticut. She is a Licensed Master Social Worker and lives in Connecticut. Connect with Tina on LinkedIn.

One Woman's Voyage to Triumph

ANGELA JOHNSON

I AM FREE! As I embrace this FREEDOM that I have been so graciously given, allow me to be transparent as I acknowledge that I was bound in so many ways until a few years ago. I attended a night service at church and the officiating minister walked over to me after her sermon and softly whispered in my ear "YOU ARE FREE." God will send the right people at the opportune time to accomplish His will. Although circumstances arise from time to time, I hold on to that truth...I AM FREE! The shackles are off! "Who the Son sets free is free indeed."

"Journey's been rough, Lord knows it's been tough, but you're still here." These lyrics minister to me daily. My life has been, to say the least, a series of storms; twists and turns; peaks and valleys; but still short of a Euroclydon. I know what it means to be God–centered and anchored.

Many of my experiences influenced choices I made, and behaviors I embodied along the way. Yet, my resiliency would always allow me to rise up, bounce back, and above all overcome challenges and circumstances that were never meant to harm me. Instead, they were used to develop me, "prosper me, and give me a hope and a future."

It all began when He thought of me, formed me, and blessed my mom to give birth to me in August 1960. Unfortunately, my mom passed the day after she gave birth to me, at the tender age of 14 from childbirth complications. The thought of my mom giving her life to save my own, just as Jesus did, often crosses my mind. It does not surprise me since she was often described as the protector of her family and loved ones. What a sacrifice! This, in and of itself confirms that God has PURPOSE and PLANS for my life that has yet to be fully manifested. RIP Mom. I will continue to protect, but it is a different kind of fight.

I was raised by one of the most loving people I have ever known. She is my late grandmother, affectionately known as Momma. Momma embraced me as if she had given birth to me. So much so, that I remember waking up on Sunday mornings to the smell of fresh baked biscuits and the tunes of Shirley Caesar, and Momma singing,

"For the nine months I carried you, growing inside of me…NO CHARGE. When you add it all up, the full cost of my love is NO CHARGE". It is tough to resist the tears when I think of such moments, as there were many of these priceless moments. But God…

I have always loved and cared for people. As a young girl, I sought love and acceptance from others. I recall asking my third-grade teacher if she liked black girls. Her response was, "I like black girls, white girls, brown girls, and yellow girls. I love all colors." I think that was a moment of validation for me. One way I showed love was through sharing whatever I had with people regardless of their need. Many viewed this as a sign of weakness, but I admired that trait about myself. I was selfless and more concerned about taking care of others, than I was about myself. I took my education for granted, because I was so caught up in pleasing others. In middle school, particularly eighth grade, I became so distracted that I lost interest in school. I would do just enough to pass to the next grade. This pattern continued throughout high school. I did not want to disappoint my mom, and to save myself the embarrassment, I studied and completed just enough schoolwork to graduate with my high school class. God's grace saw me through!

On Monday, September 28, 1992, my life was changed forever. Nothing that I had gone through in my life could have prepared me for the phone call I would receive on this day. It was what appeared to be a typical Monday morning. We went through our normal routine. I began preparing for work, woke my 3 year old son up, and got him ready for preschool. Arriving at work at 8:30 a.m., suddenly, I felt a burden of heaviness. It was a weird feeling, but nothing I could explain. I went to the restroom not wanting anyone to see me. It was just a few days prior, I had lost my uncle but yet and still this feeling was very different when I learned of his passing. The tears began to flow. My heart became even heavier and I was crying. I was in the restroom for approximately ten minutes before my co-worker, friend walked in. Seeing me wiping my face, she asked if I was okay. Nodding my head in the affirmative, we walked back to our respective work spaces.

The call came in at approximately 10:30 a.m. It was my sister on the other end, calling to let me know that I needed to get down to New York, because mommy and daddy are dead! Worriedly I asked, "was it an accident?" Her reply was, "daddy killed mommy, and then killed himself." I vaguely remember my reactions afterwards. However, I do remember yanking the phone out of the wall. The rest was a blur.

After making arrangements for my 3 year old to be cared for, we began the dreadful journey to New York, which is where my dad and stepmom lived. While my husband drove, my sister's voice played in my head over and over like a skipping record player. This had to be a big mistake! This could NOT be real! Was this a sick scene from a movie? How would I tell my 3 year old that his papa and nana were gone?

After everyone was put to rest, as one could imagine, the emotions of grief and loss felt like a roller coaster ride. I went through guilt, anger, and depression. I was stuck in denial and acceptance for what seemed like a lifetime. I isolated from the outside world while signs of emotional instability showed up impacting my marriage, as well as other relationships. My oldest son even started to exhibit behaviors that were uncharacteristic of him.

18 long, hard years past before I could honestly say I accepted the loss. Up until then, not a day went by without me shedding tears related to the tragedy. That was a huge breakthrough for me. Although I will never get that time back, I can say that the lessons learned on my journey are much greater than the pain my experiences caused me. There was an awakening!

This theme of trials and tragedies had become too commonplace in my life. One evening while listening to the message from a speaker, "you do not need another experience, but a new perspective," resonated with me. "Thinking that has brought me this far has created some problems that this thinking cannot solve." It was time to change my "stinking thinking," and focus on what was ahead and not behind me. My past experiences were to be used to transform my life. I had been broken, but I was being stitched back together. I am now more aware of what life is revealing to me. And, I am more careful to not miss the lessons along the way!

A new lesson of self-discovery began in January 2013 when I enrolled in a substance abuse and addictions counseling training program offered by Department of Mental Health and Addiction Services (DMHAS). While training to become an addiction counselor, I was challenged to do self-reflections, and ultimately to face the "man in the mirror." I learned what my biases, strengths, and weaknesses were. It helped me become culturally sensitive, aware, and competent. I became less judgmental. Knowing who I am and how I am influenced by culture and beliefs helped me better serve others more effectively. This training program also prepared me for higher learning.

After completing the program at DMHAS, I enrolled in the Human Services program at Springfield College. Although I had experienced some struggles with memory loss due to the trauma, I did not let this prevent me from pursuing a degree. One of the courses I registered for was, "Coping with Death and Disease." This course was also very instrumental in helping me overcome my process of grieving my losses. A little delayed, but not denied. There were many challenges along the way. I lost my momma, the only one that I knew, in my second semester of college. Yet determined, I earned a Bachelor of Science degree in Human Services in May 2018. I believed I could, so I did! I learned some years ago that I was anointed, and that my anointing came with a huge price. I was called to do something greater in this life.

One early Friday evening in September 2019, after dinner with a dear girlfriend of mine, she deviated from the route we normally took, which delayed us arriving on my street by five minutes. As we turned onto my street, a man was signaling for help. I heard what sounded like a faint cry for help, but my girlfriend said she heard what sounded like a scream for help. Without hesitation, she stopped her vehicle, put it in park, and we both jumped out to assist the panicking man whose friend was pinned underneath his vehicle. The three of us attempted to lift the vehicle. It barely moved! My girlfriend dialed 911, while I knelt down near the body that was pinned under the car and began to call out to God for help as I recited scriptures. As I later, screamed for help, a passerby in a truck jumped out to assist. Paramedics arrived soon after. Four men, including the Emergency Medical Technicians (EMTs), lifted the vehicle and was able to bring the body to safety. As I reflect on that moment, I realized the BLESSING of miracles!

I have listened to Bishop T.D. Jakes for many years and gleaned from him an abundance of spiritual knowledge and wisdom encompassing purpose and destiny, amongst a plethora of other topics! I am ready for my God-given gifts to be unleashed so that I can effectively help others.

As I continue to emerge on my journey to success, I am finding answers to questions I once had, "Why am I here?" I am a willing vessel, always ready to be used by God. I will go wherever He wants me to go and do whatever He wants me to do. It is my hope that my experiences and testimonies will be used for the greater good, such as helping others overcome, and become healed and whole. The Potter has uniquely formed his clay and delights in putting our broken pieces back together. We were all born on purpose with purpose for God to use. We are equipped with everything we need to accomplish our "God-size" goals. "All things work together for the good of those who love the Lord, and who are called according to His purpose." "With God, ALL things are possible!" Be ENCOURAGED, be POSITIVE, and be BLESSED!

About the Author

Angela Johnson is married with five adult sons and adorable grandchildren. She is a Certified Life Coach, with an emerging perfectly imperfect model coaching business. She is gifted and skilled at encouraging, inspiring, and empowering others to tap into their unrealized dreams and possibilities. She is also called to do spiritual mentoring. She would love to connect with you via email @ johnsad579@sbcglobal.net.

Don't Pause on Life

TRISHAUNA JOHNSON

"We need women who are so strong they can be gentle, so educated they can be humble, so fierce they can be compassionate, so passionate they can be rational, and so disciplined they can be free."

— Kavita Ramdas

When I was younger, there were commercials of young white girls happily celebrating their menstrual cycle as if it was a rite of passage to womanhood. They always appeared so bubbly and thrilled about being on their period and enjoyed all of life's activities. It was no struggle for them but rather like celebrating a chance to be photographed for a magazine cover. This was no badge of honor for me as a black girl raised in the housing projects of New Orleans. I dreaded IT! Being the fourth born of six, I was not ready to trade in my high top All-Star tennis shoes or tomboy lifestyle for the rite of passage to womanhood. I had other plans!

Furthermore, in my generation, to speak of such things that involved a woman's body was taboo. It was not customary in my culture to have an open dialogue about our *personal* matters. You lived and you learned as life unfolded the details. Don't get me wrong; there were times when my mother would pass on some life advice or riddle. I would hear things like, "don't let those boys touch you"..." if you kiss a boy, you'll get pregnant." Did YOU ever hear such things? Let me tell you a little more about my journey as a young black woman going from menstruation to menopause.

"PMS: Prepare to Meet Satan."

— Unknown

My visitor came unannounced when I was in the 6th grade. At the time, I didn't know much about (her) menstruation. I quickly learned that she would be visiting every 28 days, like clock-work. I thought she was selfish as she wanted to me lie around with heating pads, taking pain relievers, trying to ease the discomfort she brought with her. Like most young girls, I learned to adjust to my changing body. As I matured into womanhood, I did not realize yet another phase would manifest itself. No one ever told me that your menstrual cycle ceases, and a new intruder named menopause would take over with its unique selfish wants!

What comes to mind when you hear the word menopause?

Most people might think of menopause as a disease for cranky old women, antiquated myths, unpleasant mood swings, and loss of sex drive. Others may draw a blank conclusion because it is not on their radar. I guess menopause is one of those topics, like religion and politics, and the headliner of TURNING 40, that you don't want talk about it.

My older sister was like a walking billboard for menopause. I laugh as I think of times when she would announce to whoever that would listen as she proclaimed, "Oh my God, I'm having a hot flash!" According to Medical News Today, "the frequency of hot flashes and night sweats differ between people. Some only experience occasional hot flashes while, for others, the symptoms can get in the way of daily life."

The winter in Minnesota feels like the North Pole, especially when you're from a warm area like New Orleans. My younger sister's husband thought she was going insane when she would sleep with the window open while running the fan in the blistery Minnesota winter! I have to say, I have been fortunate that my menopause symptoms were not that extreme.

When I was 45, I started to suspect that my body's rhythm was out of sync. The quiet but not so meek visitor began to erupt like a volcano with a heavy flow. The symptoms would rage like a war on my body and mood. I remember being aware of the awkward moment that something had changed. By the time I was 47, I had thought it would be best to seek advice from my doctor as I continued to notice changes in my mood. I shared my concerns that I suspected that I might be going through menopause. However, my white female doctor looked at me and said, "No, you are too young to be going through menopause." I realized at this moment that I needed more information about the experiences of African-American women and menopause. Did our bodies go through changes differently from our white counterparts? I heard the words that fell from my doctor's lips, but I KNEW what I was feeling and experiencing. There were times when I would wake up in pools of water from night sweats. On one occasion, I was out with some friends, and everyone started asking me if I was okay, with alarming looks on their faces. I responded, "Yes, I'm okay," but became perplexed as to why I was being asked this question. Little did I realize I had been sweating profusely. But on the inside, I felt fine.

The effects of menopause made me feel unstable. One minute I was on fire, and the next minute, I was ice cold. One minute, I was calm, and the next minute, I was climbing a wall. The waves would come so fast! I didn't know whether to strip my clothes off *or* keep them on. I had mixed emotions as I was transitioning into another chapter of life. I was happy that I would no longer have a monthly intruder and sad that I didn't know what to expect. I had more questions than answers. I could not solicit help from my mother because she had a hysterectomy in her early 30's and no aid from my doctor, who thought I was too young to experience menopause.

Armed with night sweats and no support from my doctor, I did what I always have done. I researched to gain more knowledge about my situation with particular attention to African-American women. Unfortunately, I didn't find much information, but I discovered natural solutions to reduce some of the symptoms. The symptoms of menopause can last for years and can affect each woman differently. Menopause can be treated in various ways like hormone therapy, Chinese medicine, homeopathy, acupuncture, or herbal treatments to reduce the symptoms.

Herbal treatment

I chose to use herbs to relieve night sweats and other menopausal symptoms. I felt more comfortable using herbs because they are less invasive, with less chances of becoming addictive like some prescribed medications, and there are fewer chances of harmful side effects. According to Verywell Health, the use of Black Cohosh can be an effective treatment for certain symptoms, including hot flashes and mood swings. It also has a good safety record and may be a great first choice if you want to try something besides estrogen to treat your hot flashes. The U.S. National Center for Complementary and

Integrative Medicine has a fact sheet about the supplement that you may find helpful.

I used Black Cohosh to reduce night sweats and Red Clover to reduce other symptoms of menopause. Ultimately, you are responsible for your health and talking with your health care provider about any health approaches that may be beneficial for you. Together, you can make the best decisions for your unique experiences. According to the Indian Theory of Existence, "Everything on the earth has a purpose, every disease an herb to cure it, and every person a mission."

I used walking and biking as my means of exercise to relieve some of my symptoms and to ease any discomfort I might have experienced. Exercise is good for your mental health. It benefits your bones and develops a stronger heart. A healthy diet also plays a big part in easing your symptoms. "The greatest discovery of any generation is that human beings can alter their lives by altering their attitudes of mind."

— Albert Schweitzer

I conducted a short questionnaire with females and one male Facebook subscriber to find out what they knew or heard about menopause. In my findings, many did not know much about menopause regardless of race, age, or economic status. One subscriber said menopause "its hell, you are hot, you are cold, your mouth is extremely dry and you think that a cool breeze will save you but hope nothing and you get ready for a hell-storm, extra weight and more". Another subscriber said, "Lawd, it was crazy."

I aspire to empower women to start early on their quest to learn about menopause and to embrace the process. Menopause is a natural evolution in a woman's life. She is emerging internally and externally. I invite you to embrace a more positive outlook about menopause. It is not the end of the story. It is just the beginning of the next chapter. In the 1930s, menopause was given such a negative connotation, like a deficiency disease. Today, we know much more. We have many more tools, resources, options, and education to address how our bodies may respond to the changes.

From Menstruation to Menopause, our rites of passage as women are only part of who we are. We are educated, liberated, and celebrated along this journey called life. I ask you, "Are you continuing to celebrate this chapter of your life?" I haven't let the physical or emotional changes of menopause to halt my dreams and goals of inspiring and empowering other women. It has helped me to better connect with them. As I emerge in this chapter of my life, I leave you with some things to consider to support your voyage...

Maintain a gratitude journal celebrating the benefits that come with menopause. Take inventory of what is meaningful during this stage of life. Focus on self-care. It is your time to celebrate you.

Network with other menopausal women, share stories and exchange coping strategies. Celebrate the changes in this chapter of life.

About the Author

Trishauna Johnson is the proud owner of Resilient by Design LLC., Certified Coach and Speaker who is affectionately known as the "SnappBack Coach." She is no stranger to struggles and trauma. Raised in New Orleans housing projects now living in Minnesota, Trishauna has spent her adult life helping others recover from messy life storms.

Trishauna has tapped into her many years of life experience to craft her message of resilience. Her audiences have tremendously benefited from her lessons of hope, faith, and resiliency that she shares with humor and sass. She is a Mental Health Practitioner, presently serving at an Intensive Residential Treatment Services & Crisis Facility. She holds a Master's Degree in Rehabilitation Counseling from Minnesota University in Mankato. She has an adult son; and is the hands-on G mama of two energetic grandsons. Connect with Trishauna at resilientbydesigncoaching@gmail.com or

www.snappbackcoach.com or www.facebook.com/snappbackcoach

Don't Drink It!

Leah Lueck

Do you ever stop to think about what you think about? That might sound like a funny question, but it's not really. Let me explain why.

First, let me introduce myself. I am mom to my son Kyle, who is the best gift I've ever been given. I am enjoying a successful career in the Information Technology (IT) world, as a data analyst and have my own coaching business, Living Beyond Average, in which I have the privilege of assisting people in designing tailor-made lives and businesses. I am truly excited about my life and future; however, I can tell you, it wasn't always this way.

I'm sure some of you can relate to the narrative of growing-up in my era: go to school, get a good education, get a good job, and retire comfortably. Well, I bought that Kool-Aid and drank it! I remember when I first started my job thinking: I will only be here five years and then venture out to do "what I really want to do". You see, considering myself a "people-person", I envisioned working with people rather than on a computer all day. However, one year led to five, which led to 10, which led to 20 and somewhere the flame of who I was and my heart's desire grew so dim, I actually felt I lost myself and forgot my dreams.

I don't know about you, but I learned all too quickly that parts of adulting suck—like paying bills, responsibilities, obligations, ...etc. There's the mortgage, the car note, utility bills...OH! Then children come along. Though you wouldn't trade them for the world, they want to eat! Life became: "I owe! I owe! So off to work I go!". And, life starts throwing darts at you that you have to dodge as you try to keep all the plates of commitment spinning. In my case, I married the man of my dreams—ending in divorce court—and had to keep those plates spinning. During my marriage, I experienced multiple miscarriages, later my mother passed away and a business deal went south. All the while, I kept dodging the darts while trying to keep the plates spinning. How about you? Do you have your own version of plate-spinning?

I woke up one day, realizing 25 years had passed in what seemed to be the blink of an eye. I asked myself, "Is this life? Is this really all there is to life?" To me, it seemed the wind created by all the plate-spinning and dart-dodging, blew-out my candles before I even got to make my wish, feeling as if my dreams, my "flame" extinguished. The reason: I bought and drank the Kool-Aid. I even called out to God for a reminder of what my dreams were.

Though I entered my IT career due to my degree in statistics, my degree in psychology better reflected my real passion: understanding human behavior and helping people. It was around the time of calling out to God that I came across a book by Dana Wilde, entitled Train Your Brain.[1] Within this book, Dana told the story of an HBO documentary about the lives of people with Dissociative Identity Disorder (DID), also known as Multiple Personality Disorder. She relayed the story of a lady named Barb, who presented with multiple personalities.

One day Barb, her husband, and two daughters, went grocery shopping. It appeared to be a rather regular shopping experience until, in the cereal aisle, Barb started speaking in the voice of a five-year old girl and told her husband about a certain cereal she wanted. In this personality, she was known as Mae. Seeming to have difficulty seeing clearly, her husband assisted her in removing the glasses she was wearing, as Mae was unable to see properly with Barb's glasses.

The documentary did not provide any explanation as to whether Barb's eyesight had a physiological change with the change in personality. It did, however, send Dana on a quest to seek out a greater understanding of the phenomenon. Dana learned that there are medically documented cases that stated instances in which, in one personality, a person may have a scar or a bruise which vanished when they slipped into another personality. Additionally, some will change eye color as their personality changes.

This phenomenon amazed me. I wondered: What power does the mind have and how much of it do we leave lying dormant in our regular day-to-day lives? If true physiological changes can happen in an instant, within the same body, it is hard for me to believe that a person would truly have to undergo a personality change for that to happen. Again, I wondered: What does this mean for you and me?

While we may not need some physiological change in our bodies, is there power within the mind that we can plug into, to create desired changes in other aspects of our lives? While you may not have "lost" yourself, nor lost sight of your dreams and goals, most of us have some aspect of our lives that we desire to be different. It seems; however, we often grapple with the "how-to" of change.

Let's go back to my original question: Do you ever stop to think about what you think about? The study of human behavior suggests that the majority of our day, we run on auto-pilot. This means that we are performing tasks by habit or muscle memory rather than actually consciously giving any thought to what we are doing.[2] For example: Have you ever thrown a load of wash into the dryer and questioned, if just 20 seconds earlier, you added in the fabric softener sheet? Autopilot!! If we give so little thought to the majority of our days, is it any wonder that although we have a desire for change, we rarely experience it?

Albert Einstein said, "We cannot solve our problems with the same thinking we used when we created them." Basically, if you want something different, you are going to have to think something different. Here is a big "why" to that: There is a part of our brain known as the Reticular Activating System (RAS) that helps us stay "sane" by filtering the millions of bytes of information that we take in. It deems things as "important" or "not important" at a particular time.[3] It selects and presents information as "important" based on what you think about and talk about. If you are giving attention to something, the RAS believes that that is "important" to you. The RAS's filtering system then assists in matching-up incoming data with your thoughts.

Here is an example of the RAS's filtering system at work. Let's imagine you went car shopping. You saw a new red-hot corvette and knew that it had your name on it so you buy it. As you start driving around town, you begin to notice a number of red-hot corvettes all around you. My question to you: Do you think that these cars all came out after you bought yours? Probably not, but prior to you buying the car, your RAS did not bring them to your attention. If you currently have a problem and you keep talking and thinking about the problem, your RAS is going to do its job and find all kinds of evidence to support your problem and present it back to you. This results in reinforcing the problem even further in your mind.

Additionally, the RAS can present information that can appear to "confirm" thoughts. These thoughts then appear "real"—even though they may not be "true". Things like: "I'm too old"; "I'm so fat"; "it's too late for me"; "no one likes me"; "everything I try fails"—and so on. Therefore, to resolve the problem, you have to do as Einstein suggests: change your thinking; change from thinking about the problem to finding the solution.

Another fascinating aspect of the mind is that it cannot distinguish between something happening in reality and something imagined. You can create the same physiological effects by imagining something—as if it actually happened. Try this: Sit back, and imagine holding in your hand, half of a cool, perfectly shaped yellow lemon. See it clearly in your mind. Now, go ahead and bite into it. What did you experience? If you are like many, your body would have reacted the way it does when you actually eat something sour: your mouth may have puckered-up or you might have made a grimacing face, even started to salivate. Most likely, it caused you to react even though you simply imagined it.

When imagining, there are two other factors that influence the level of your body's response: the degree to which you participate in the imagining and whether or not there is a strong emotional component to it. I doubt any of us would have really been emotionally "charged" with this little experiment. However, regarding life in general, the more emotion that is equated with an event, the greater the memory and physiological response created.[4] So, the more emotion you can elicit even to an imagined event, the more "real" that imagination can become.

As I applied these concepts to my life, I realized I could either bemoan my past and all the years I had not pursued my dreams or I could take control of my thoughts and intentions and point them in the direction which I desired to experience in my life. As I started to work with coaches and enrolled in personal development courses, those mere smoldering embers of my long-held dreams re-emerged. It felt as if I was being "re-introduced" to Leah, not Leah "the wife", "the ex-", "the mom", the "IT guru". I was able to rediscover Leah, the lover of life and of people! I realized I did not have to continue to drink the Kool-Aid. I could change the narrative, update my RAS with what is important to me and start moving in a new direction. I could employ an emotionally charged imagination to help me create the life I desired rather than replay my past.

As I did this, doors of opportunity for preparation began to open. I learned how to craft my story, which led to me joining a challenge to go live on Facebook for 21 days. Then, invitations started to come for live speaking engagements, guest appearances on radio shows and Facebook interviews and the opportunity to contribute to this book... Emerging.

So, one final time I ask you: Do you ever stop to think about what you think about? Are your thoughts taking you in the direction of your dreams and goals?

No matter what age you are, remember: it is not too late, and you are not too old to start living a life you are passionate about; a life that makes you excited to get up in the morning and still have gas in your tank when you go to bed! Your passion may be something you turn into profit or may simply be something you do for pleasure. Either way, I hope you join me in this awesome adventure of life by choosing to think about what you think about—and then choose to Live Beyond Average.

1. Wilde, Dana. Train Your Brain. Balboa Press, 2013
2. Szegedy-Maszak, Marianne. "Mysteries of the mind Your unconscious is making your everyday decisions", http://webhome.auburn.edu/~mitrege/ENGL2210/USN WR-mind.html
3. "Reticular Activating System: Definition & Function." Study.com, 23 August 2016, https://study.com/academy/lesson/reticular-activating-system-definition-function.html
4. McPherson, Dr. Fiona. "The Role of Emotion in Memory", https://www.memory-key.com/memory/emotion#

About the Author

Leah Lueck is an entrepreneur, life and business coach, song-writer, and health & wellness enthusiast. More importantly, Leah is a proud mom, honored to be called a friend and thrives on being an encourager of others. She is an avid learner and enjoys gleaning all she can on an expansive array of topics. For more information about her and Living Beyond Average, visit: www.LeahLueck.com; FB@Living Beyond Average or on LinkedIn.

The Release

UNEDRA MULEY

NUMBNESS:

Finally made it home after a long day. First thing I wanted to do was to jump on the couch and ball-up in a fluffy blanket. I walk into the kitchen and realize that the dishes needed to be washed. The battle in my head begun. Should I wash them now or do I wash them later? This played over-and-over in my head, but the couch lost that battle and I stood there at the sink washing away. All of a sudden, I heard two words that would change my world forever, "I'm leaving." What? Leaving? What did this all mean? Did I actually hear these words, or did I really jump onto the couch and fall fast asleep into the beginning stages of a bad dream? No. I wasn't dreaming. At that very moment when these words were said, I was holding a knife in my hand. My first thought was to throw the knife and all of this would be over. In a flash, all of these emotions exploded in my head at one time and the only thing I could feel was total numbness. I just stood there as my world, that I once knew, was crumbling around me. A few years later, I walked out of the court house - divorce finalized.

BELIEVING THE LIE OF THE ENEMY:

The thief comes only in order to steal, kill and destroy. I came that they may have and enjoy life, and have it in abundance (to the full, till it overflows).

— John 10:10 AMP

What day is this? I could not tell you how long I have been in this bed. Am I still alive? I hear a baby crying. Boxes and boxes of tissue lie on the floor. Couldn't hardly see out of my eyes because they were swollen shut. No more tears to cry. Food? What food? Who can eat? My feet hit the floor. I can't even stand. I don't want to stand. How did I get here? The torment of the devil has begun. I heard his words and believed every single lie of the enemy - self-doubt, rejection, low self-esteem, unworthiness, unwanted, useless. The list goes on and on. I felt the heaviness of my circumstance - the trial of the storm. As author, Leif Hetland, has written, the enemies' strategies are not new. They are very predictable, and they seem to work every time, until we realize what he is up to. It's time to wake up to his strategies. He will try to create confusion about your future.

THE STAGES YOU MAY EXPERIENCE:

Through all of this, you cannot ignore that the stages of grief are real. You may face denial, anger, bargaining, depression, and acceptance. Whatever you have experienced in life, you may have transitioned into one or more of these stages. At one point, these stages became my best friend. They can't be ignored and if you find that you need help in these areas, please reach out to a counselor, community services, or church in your area. Processing and getting it all out, will help out in the end.

ATMOSPHERE SHIFT:

So tired. Now what? I knew that I could not do this by myself and I dropped to my knees and cried out to the Lord. "Help Me Jesus." The sound that came from my mouth was so deep and unfamiliar. It was a desperate cry from the deepest part of my being. I heard a soft voice. I looked around the room – no one was there. Hello? I knew I heard something. I must be so tired that I think I am now hearing voices. Sleep is what I need. Definitely hours of sleep. I tried to go back to sleep.......There it was again – a soft voice that kept saying, Isaiah 41:10. I shot straight up in my bed – realizing who was speaking. There was no loud voice, no thunderous-booming noise or sound of a trumpet. It was a small quiet voice that told me to get up and read a scripture in the Bible....God heard my cry and spoke in such a loving way. He led me to a scripture on this 10th day of March, 2006 at 3:00am (EST):

So, do not fear, for I am with you; do not be dismayed, for I am your God. I will strengthen you and help you; I will uphold you with my righteous right hand.

— Isaiah 41:10 NIV

When you think that you have nothing left, God shows up in a mighty way. That was all I needed to know that He was there with me. I went to bed that night not knowing what my next move was going to be. I woke up energized and empowered. The sleepless nights soon turned to restful joy. I soon began to realize that the mountain that blocked me had crumbled down into mere pebbles. The internal shift had begun!

WARRIORS RISE AND TAKE YOUR PLACE:

No matter what life challenges you face or things that overwhelm you, we can stand through the storm. God is here and will never leave your side. At times, you may think that you will not make it and find yourself sliding backwards - right back at step 1. That step of listening to the negative voices. Building up the walls and standing there staring at them. No! Do not listen to the enemy. Do not listen to the lies that he will try and tell you. You have an assignment. God has created you for such a time as this (Book of Esther). Things that you have gone through are only for a season – they make you stronger, help create who you are. You can stand the fire. Just like in the Book of Daniel. Shadrach, Meshack, and Abednego were thrown into the fire by Nebuchadnezzar, but when everyone looked inside the fiery furnace, they saw a 4th person walking in the flames. You too will go through the trials of fire, but you are protected. Remember this is just a test – a moment in life.

The Lord is my rock, my fortress and my deliverer; my God is my rock, in whom I take refuge. He is my shield and the horn of my salvation, my stronghold.

— Psalm 18:2 NIV

He will never give you anything that you can't bear. So, stand firm in who God has created you to be. If you find that you are still stuck, if you have lost someone, divorce, or face other mountains – this is your time to stand – rise up and put your feet on the ground. You can do this!

HIGHEST PRAISE:

Enjoying life as it is now. That was a chapter in my life that despite the emotional rollercoaster, I have embraced that season. As others are facing similar situations, I'm offering my testimony of overcoming a time in my life. As it says in Joshua 6, shout down your own Jericho wall (whatever that wall may be). Give all the glory to God. Walk in your assignment. You have so much more to do in life.

Let the Lord speak and change your atmosphere. The labels of your past are washed away. Believe in yourself. There are no limits to what you can do.

ENJOYING LIFE:

Enjoying life and waiting to see what He has for me next. As I step into another season of my life – I'm embracing all that God has to offer. I may not know exactly what the next step will be, but I'm believing and trusting. I feel the joyfulness of all that God has. He is preparing the way and I will enjoy every moment of it. As people mourn being an empty nester, I jump for joy with excitement about this journey I am on. The doors that will be opening, the world I will see, the new people that will come into my life, job opportunities, are just a few things that I may experience. Will there be ups and downs? Of course! But I know that God is with me and no matter what comes my way, I'm standing with the Lord. So, let's go and get moving....come dance with me as I dance my way into another chapter. Who is coming with me? Get on board so we can all hear......Well done my faithful servant.

ADDITIONAL RESOURCES:

By Leif Hetland

You may not know me, but I know everything about you

Psalm 139

I know when you sit down and when you rise up.

Psalm 139:2

I am familiar with all your ways.

Psalm 139:3

Even the very hairs on your head are numbered.

Matthew 10:29-31

In me you live and move and have your being

Acts 17:28

If you receive the gift of my son Jesus, you receive me.

1 John 2:23

My questions is…Will you be my child?

John 1:12-13

I am waiting for you

Luke 15:11-32

About the Author

Unedra Muley is from New Haven, Connecticut and attends Gateway Christian Fellowship and is very active within her church community. She is also a co-chair of The National Liturgical Dance Network - CT Chapter, which she has ministered all over in-state and out-of-state for church functions or conferences. Unedra has two Masters, one of which is a Licensed Master Social Worker. She has worked for a State Agency since 1994, and is enjoying every moment with her son. Unedra hopes that you have been blessed by the words in this chapter and the testimony was life changing. Connect with Unedra via Facebook.

Breaking the Silence

MARIAN PEYNADO

Oh, how I loved to hear the tooting of that horn as it came around the corner up the hill to stop at the bottom of my Great Grandmother's gate. The sound, so distinct, I knew whose car it was, who would be driving and sitting in the passenger seat. Once I heard that horn, I'd immediately stop what I was doing. My eyes lit up, my heart leaped with joy and my feet ran to the front yard prancing as I waited for the car to pull up. When I saw it, I gasped as the mulatto toned man who stood six inches over five feet opened the passenger door, stepped out, taking off his hat to show his half bald head. He smiled at me and I smiled back. Then with arms wide open, I ran down the hill screaming Daddy! He picked me up, we hugged, and he carried me up the hill into the yard. My head rested on his shoulders; I took a deep breath inhaling the scent of Brut which reassured me this was not a surreal moment.

These precious moments from my childhood, I will forever cherish, for unbeknownst to me they would be short lived. People often enter our lives leaving footprints. However, the indentation each footprint leaves differs. For some, it is as though they have been cemented- leaving their mark in our lives forever or for as long as we allow them to. When the people we have the utmost respect and love for, hurt us and are no longer a part of our lives, the effects can give birth to a whirlwind of emotions leaving one tormented with depression, self-hate, and anger. We are left trying to answer the Who? What? And why of those fine details of our lives so we can arrive at a place of peace.

I was seven years old. The moment I had been anxiously waiting for had finally come. My dad visited me every year sometimes twice a year. My cousin Mr. P, his driver, usually followed us up the hill holding two suitcases filled with toys and clothing for me. This time he only had one small suitcase. I wasn't sure why at the moment, but that didn't matter. With him he brought the scent of America. Whenever he visited, that's when the fun began. At seven years old, I had already visited the fourteen parishes of Jamaica.

Daddy and I took road trips to various tourist attractions on the island. The Boston Jerk Pit was our all-time favorite spot. Merchant stalls with an array of native fruits and handcrafted souvenirs adorned the street sides. I saw folding waters with white trimmings rushing to meet its pebble filled lover sitting under the sun, laying bare, forever waiting to be kissed. Once we arrived at the Boston Jerk Pit, my seven-year-old tummy would be satisfied by smoked jerk pork and chicken marinated in scotch bonnet pepper, thyme, pimento, the finest of spices smoked over green pimento wood, infused by the charcoal beneath. We would visit family in the Parish of St. Elizabeth and take boat rides on the famous black river. We visited caves, climbed waterfalls and took hot mineral baths under showers flowing from an extinct volcano. Unbeknownst to my daddy, he had created a little lady who loves to travel. I dreamt of us traveling the world together.

I would later find out that reason my cousin had only one small suitcase was because this would be my dad's final trip where he wouldn't leave me behind. I was ecstatic to know that, "I AM GOING TO AMERICA!" I can recall with the biggest smile on my face and telling my friends. The days of me daydreaming in anticipation of being on a plane had finally come to an end. I would now be going on a plane with my daddy, the man I admired most, to the Big Apple- NEW YORK CITY!

It was March. New York was cold in comparison to the hot years I've spent under the sun in Jamaica. Daddy introduced me to all his friends and family members I had no knowledge of. He took me on train rides to tour Manhattan, visited the Statue of Liberty and my birthday would be spent on boat rides around the New York Harbor.

A struggling student, I was taken from the 2nd grade and placed in a first-grade class. Daddy's girlfriend was once an elementary teacher in Jamaica, hence evenings after school would be spent with her for extra lessons. Soon, I would become an honor student. Daddy often compared me to one of my older brothers who was now a grown man and old enough to be my father. He told me of how bright my brother was "your brother could do his homework in front of a TV without being distracted and complete it in no time." Daddy spoke highly of my brother and I regarded him as the man with the intellectual capacity I too would have. He had huge shoes for me to fill.

In Jamaica we have a saying "Si mi and live wid mi a two different ting,"[1] the statement proved to me it's truthfulness once I started living with my dad. The man I longed to be with would soon become the man I feared and hated. When I did something that was not to his liking, daddy would call me dumb. Followed by, "yuh[2] stupid ass yuh." When I ate, I was told "yuh a get too fat; yuh nyam tu much."[3] In those moments, I longed for my mother's comfort far beyond my reach. Separated by the sea, all I wanted was my mom!

Daddy allowed me to stay up late watching Western movies with him. One night instead of the usual western movie, the TV was

---

1. Seeing me and living with me are very different.

2 . You

3 . You are getting to fat; you eat too much.

turned to "La Femme Nakita." As I sat on the caramel toned seventies style swivel chair, a feeling of discomfort beheld me. I knew the content of this particular show was not for a child my age. I no longer saw my daddy as a noble man. I looked over and he was sitting on the couch, eyes glued to the television. I wanted to get up but somehow, I felt frozen. Wanted to say good night but for some reason the words couldn't make their way out. That night daddy offered to tuck me in bed. Again, I wanted to say no, but the word "ok" came from my lips.

My room was dark with no night light. Daddy tucked me in, then laid on the left side of my bed behind me with his hand over my waist. He then started rubbing on my belly. Each time he rubbed; it was as though my shirt was being lifted. Soon daddy was rubbing on my skin. As he rubbed, I could feel his hands get higher. To the right of me was my teddy, I held him close; thinking somehow, he could save me from the discomfort I was feeling. It just didn't feel right. I remember wishing daddy would just leave my room! I asked myself "Why didn't you say no to him putting you to bed?" Whilst I silently reprimanded myself, I clenched teddy as tight as I could. For some reason I thought instead of rubbing mine, he would rub teddy's belly. Teddy was as helpless as I. Left with nothing but silent screams and cold tears rolling down my cheeks, four years, I did nothing but smile.

The man I once loved, I now despised and wanted to die. One morning after daddy woke me up for school, as usual I went to the bathroom and as usual, I fell asleep on the toilet with my head rested on the cold, tiled, bathroom wall. On this particular morning, I sat naked on the toilet. So tired, I didn't hear him knocking. Soon I was awakened by the sound of the bathroom door being shoved open. I would be pulled from the toilet seat, into the hallway to feel scraps of leather whipping against my skin. I screamed and cried. I wanted him to stop so I wouldn't be embarrassed anymore. Puberty took its natural course for me, earlier than most. At ten years old, I was well developed, trying to cover myself as my daddy flogged me on the hallway floor. These actions left me tormented with emotions and questioning why he would treat me this way after promising a better life.

For four years I lived with my dad. The truth was unveiled after a summer of traveling to England, Wales and Jamaica, then returning home to the US. That October of 1999, daddy and I got into a fight outside my elementary school - PS.38. After that, I was determined to run away to my cousins in Connecticut. Afraid of getting lost or even kidnapped, I reconsidered. The New York Administration for Child Services became involved because of the fight we had on school grounds. I was questioned a multitude of times by officials visiting me at home and school.

A perfect opportunity for me to expose him, yet I couldn't. I was afraid for him and myself. Unbeknownst to me, amidst the investigations from ACS, daddy was being questioned by family in Jamaica about the things he had done to me. I had broken my silence to my aunt during my summer trip to Jamaica. I remember her telling me "Yuh nuh look like yuhself, yuh too sad man."[4] Then one hot summer afternoon while standing in Port Morant Square waiting at the bus stop, she looked down at me and our eyes mirrored each other. She uttered "Marian, him touch yuh?"[5] I did not respond. Again, with her eyes still mirroring mine, she said "don't lie to mi enuh!"[6] "him touch yuh?" My silence was now broken.

Breaking the silence is never easy for victims of sexual abuse and sexual violence. After years of fighting with the emotions I felt towards my dad and the person he had caused me to become, it dawned on me that I have full control of my future. What I experienced in those four years, affected me physically, emotionally, mentally, socially and sexually. With this realization, I sought clinical and spiritual guidance to heal the scars so deep and gain a wholesome feeling of freedom, peace and joy. I knew my purpose was bigger than my past, so I had to break the silence for myself and for the many women and men who are still screaming in silence to be heard, to be seen, and to be freed.

---

4. You don't look like your usual self, you very look sad.

5. Marian, he touched you?

6. Don't lie to me. The term enuh is used to emphasize the previously stated point.

About the Author

Marian Peynado was born in her great-grandmother's house, in the town of Wheelers Field and the parish of St. Thomas, Jamaica, W.I. Marian is a woman with many passions, one of which is traveling. She desires to travel for leisure and purposefully use her social work and creative art skills to restore hope in others. Breaking the Silence is Marian's first published writing, where she accounts for her experience with childhood sexual abuse.

Wonder

MARY JO TERRANOVA

"With love, with patience and with faith, she'll make her way"

Natalie Merchant, Wonder 1995 "Tiger Lily"

When I first heard this song in a yoga class, it stirred up many different emotions for me as I realized that fewer words rang truer to me. When I reflected, I realized it was because those three attributes have helped me to become more understanding of the things that are going on in the world today and the things I have experienced in my life. The song is about a child with a disability. And the refrain explains it all. *If you as parents see this child as disabled, she will be disabled. If you see her disability as a gift, she will be gifted.* God gives us all we need to live full meaningful lives and what we are missing, he makes up for with other attributes.

If not for the love of my beautiful, large and slightly dysfunctional Italian family, I would not have had the courage and confidence to "make my way." I grew up in a loving, Roman Catholic household with parents who did not have very high expectations. I am almost certain my father would have been very happy had I decided to become a Nun! Instead, I chose to become a special education teacher, a job that has been equally rewarding and frustrating. Had I known then that I would become an aunt to nieces and nephews with a varying range of disabilities, I would have been even more passionate and dedicated to the pursuit of my career. The field of special education has truly been a calling for me. I have tried to live the quote I put under my high school year book photo, almost forty years ago "What you are is God's gift to you, what you make of yourself is your gift to God." (Author unknown)

My father had significant mental health issues most of his adult life and did his best to keep them from his children until we were adults. He suffered from extreme depression and anxiety, so severe that electric shock treatments were recommended at one time. He also suffered from an extremely rare type of Obsessive Compulsive Disorder called religiosity. This disorder caused him to be obsessive regarding all of the rules, regulations and demands of the Catholic Church. If he started to say the rosary and he felt like it was not being said from the heart, he would start over. If he thought that I missed mass, a mortal sin in the church, he would pray for my eternal soul. Finding someone to treat this disorder was impossible. I mean it really was impossible. I was never able to find an expert. I searched for this person right up until my father was diagnosed with pancreatic cancer at the age of 78. Sadly, we lost him eight weeks later. Several times during my adult life, I had to admit him to a mental health facility and painfully listen as he would tell us how awful we were for what we were doing to him. I knew it was the disorder speaking, but that didn't make it any easier to hear.

My sister and her husband were married right out of high school, a concept that was completely foreign to me. At the time, I was a senior in college and relieved that my sister, who struggled greatly in school, would at least be making "her own way."

For me, having my first nephew was almost the equivalent of having my own child, without all of the sleeplessness and day to day struggles. I was allowed to be a full time loving aunt, a role I cherish to this day. Five years later, we buried our beloved Christopher Michael after a three year bout with childhood leukemia, a bone marrow transplant in Seattle and a trip to Medjugorie, Yugoslavia (circa 1990) to pray for a miracle at a place my parents believed the Blessed Virgin Mother had appeared to a group of children. Twenty years later, the pain is still there, a bit diminished and diluted but there all the same. If my level of sadness is still what it is now, what is it like for my sister and her now ex-husband?

Four more beautiful nephews followed and then two beautiful twin girls. Having so many children after losing your first born does not give you much of an opportunity to mourn or grieve properly but what happened next was completely out of the range of what I thought could happen to my beloved family.

As mental illness challenges continued to plague my family, I thought about those that weren't able to attend my special wedding day. I missed the fact that we couldn't all be together for birthday celebrations, graduations and confirmations. Holidays were always a time of additional stress and sadness and for many years, all I wanted to do was to get through them. Yet and still, "I make my way."

Many people cannot understand why I continue to maintain relationships with family members who have caused pain and sadness. For me, it was simply easier to forgive than to hold onto resentment and anger. An overabundance of love and understanding is what ultimately helped me heal.

Family trauma, displacement and addiction continued to flow through our family like wildfire. I was forced to involve the authorities in efforts to protect my parents. The situation became so bad that we eventually had to move them into a smaller apartment in an over 55 community. My mother cried the entire day we moved them out. The torn loyalties between wanting to help my parents, and my husband's strong beliefs in not enabling others was one of the most challenging things I had ever encountered. I knew my husband was right, but I was never able to convince my parents that "tough love" was the most difficult kind of love of all.

Still, love and patience have served me well. That patience manifested itself in other ways too. It has served me as a teacher, especially one who has worked with students who have challenging behaviors and difficulties regulating themselves. In my current position, I have studied as much as possible about behaviorism, truly believing that there is a function to all behaviors and the only way to change behavior is through careful consideration of "the why" behind it. Is it to avoid shame, mask insecurity or for attention they so badly need? Some of these same questions I wondered about within my family too. Did they have the support they needed? Were they masking insecurities? Living 90 miles away, afforded me the distance and time to think about how their lives could have been different.

At about the same time my family was in yet another crisis, I experienced my own miracle at the age of 41. I was a school administrator, a loving daughter and aunt. I had many close friends and a very active social life. I bought my first home and adopted a dog. I was single and ready to accept that I would be for the rest of my life. I had been through five relatively long term relationships but none of them had led to a more permanent commitment. I was not embarrassed to say that I *really did* want to be married. Yet, I continued to date men who were not capable of commitment.

However, on July 4, 2005, I met my husband Matt while at a party on Block Island, Rhode Island. That was **my** miracle. I had read every article about how I was more likely to be struck by lightning than to meet someone after the age of 40!! What I can say now? Fifteen years later, I am grateful it took me so long to find my soulmate.

My wonderful high maintenance husband was the person who even after I had been to see three therapists was finally able to help me understand my role within my family. Over the years, our cultural backgrounds have played a part in our views on family and setting healthy boundaries. Although we've had our fair share of disagreements, through it all, we find common ground in our love and respect for one another and ultimately **my love** for family. We have endured and persevered through all of our differences. We were "making our way."

I truly believe that hope and faith have led me to this current place in my life. I feel fortunate to have my wonderful family to make me stronger, my beautiful friends who were always there for me, to listen to me cry, to sympathize and to love me. I am blessed to have had friends who never judged me (you all know who you are!), supported me and laughed a lot on my wedding day!

Throughout my journey of wondering what will become of me, my siblings, nieces and nephews as we all "make our way" past the trauma, crises, disagreements and love, I know my faith has kept me.

My story of Wonder is the ability to forgive, understand and be patient with those you love. The world would be a better place if we chose love over hatred, hope over despair and joy over sadness. Remember to reflect daily on what is good in your life because it is in giving that we receive the greatest gifts in life.

To my nieces and nephews, I share my love, patience and faith. I have faith that all of you will reach your dreams and goals. The traumas and hardships have made us *all* stronger. May the memory of the love of your grandparents be in our hearts forever. Continue to "make your way."

About the Author

MaryJo Terranova currently serves as a Senior Education Specialist of the CREC Resource Group at the Capitol Region Education Council in Hartford, CT. MaryJo has been with CREC since 2011 and currently is the Director of their Advanced Alternate Route to Certification, a cross endorsement special education teacher certification program.

MaryJo earned her B.S. in Early Childhood Education from the University of Rhode Island. She holds her M.S. in Special Education from Southern Connecticut State University (SCSU). She obtained her Sixth Year Degree Diploma in both Collaboration and Consultation, and Educational Leadership from SCSU. She lives with her husband Matt in a home he built in Salem, CT. They hope to soon be the parents of several pets. Connect with MaryJo on LinkedIn.

Quitting Was Not an Option

CRYSTAL WILLIAMS

Deciding to go back to school for my Master of Social Work degree was finally making its way to becoming a reality. Having worked for the State for six years, I knew it was time but kept putting it off for some unknown reason. I talked to my husband about my decision regarding going back to school, he was very supportive and said, "go for it."

In spite of having his support and clear affirmation, I started asking myself do I really want to do this? Here I go with the negative thoughts in my head, AGAIN! So, I thought about it for *another* two weeks. I talked to a few friends about my decision. Some of them were supportive and encouraging while others were negative and asked "How are you going to do this?" "This job requires a lot of work and you will never finish your degree!" I was mad at myself for even asking their opinions. Has that ever happened to you? I said to myself "Crystal make the decision AND GET BUSY!!!!" Yet and still, I waited *another* few weeks before I applied to Springfield College.

I even asked God if I was doing the right thing. I said a prayer, kissed and blessed the envelop that fell from my hands and dropped it in the mailbox. A month later, my prayers had been answered when I received my acceptance letter. I was now on my way out of procrastination.

I was in my first year of graduate school, getting into a good rhythm as a student, full-time employee, and wife. I was learning to balance work, home and now school life. I was excited that I was easing into this routine. I was handing in my school assignments on time, not procrastinating. A theme and pattern that often came up in my life. Feeling good about myself, those negative opinions that once mattered were a distant memory.

At the end of one of my infamous long work days, I still carved out time to sit and write out a to do list for the next day. I was exhausted and looking forward to heading home on that raw, cold day. Just as I was about to pack up my things, I received a call from my brother. He was talking loud and fast like an auctioneer. He said "You gotta come home now, it's Ma, she collapsed at the bank." I asked "What do you mean?" In between his fast and pressured speech, he said "she lost a lot of blood, they're taking her to the hospital, NOW!"

I sat in my chair, body limp with a throbbing head. It felt like something hit me in the head. I could not digest what I just heard. Warm, thick tears dropped and splattered on my white blouse one by one. As I sat there motionless, I kept replaying his words over and over in my head.

Immediately, my mind went to the worst-case scenario. What if she dies? What would life be like? Have you ever been in a situation where your life just flashed before **your** eyes? Once I snapped out of it, I called my husband to explain what just happened. Knowing how I am, he asked me "Are you ok to drive right now?" I assure him I can and gather my things. The drive home felt like the longest of my life. My mind kept going back to my brother's words, that "Ma collapsed in the bank."

We arrived in Providence the next morning. All my siblings were at the hospital waiting to speak with the doctor. My mother was lying in the bed staring at all of us. I asked her how she was feeling, she smiled and said, "I'm okay". The doctor entered the room, we pounced on him as soon as he entered the doorway and started rapid firing questions at him. He politely and calmly says "your mother is a strong woman."

He explained that she lost a lot of blood and required a blood transfusion upon her arrival to the hospital. We all asked why. He looked at my mother and said Clara, "Are you okay with me telling your children what's going on with you?" She calmly says "yes." The doctor looked at us and stated "Your mother has Stage 4 Breast Cancer."

Hearing that word "CANCER" rang in my ears. All I could think of was my mother was going to DIE. I could not breathe and got very dizzy. I looked at the faces of my siblings around the room and everyone appeared in disbelief. I immediately started to pray asking God to heal my mother. My mother looked at all of us and said, in a slow but firm voice "I'm not going anywhere." I kept thinking, "What does this mean?" The doctor explained that my mother would need to start chemotherapy and radiation treatment right away. He told us that operating was not an option as the mass was too large. The prognosis was not good. She would have only 6 months to a year to live. Was I in a dream right now, did he say what I thought he said?

I remember asking my mother what she wanted to do? She said "fight" and "God was in control, not man." Leaving the hospital with a pit in my stomach, I tried to wrap my brain around the next steps and what I was going to do. The next day I went back to the hospital with what I knew was a well thought out plan to help my mother conquer her battle with cancer. I told her I was going to withdraw from school, so I could help take care of her. She looked at me in disbelief and said, "*Chris*," that is what she always called me, "quitting is not an option." I told her I could not focus on school while she was going through this. She quickly replied, "the Battle is not mine or yours, it's the Lords." She made me promise her, that I would remain in school. I agreed if she agreed to relocate to Connecticut and she did.

Adamant she did not want to live with my husband and I, she comfortably settled into her new apartment. My mother was a mentally tough lady and prided herself on her independence. The kind of person who means what they say and says what they mean. We all know people like that! She was right, though, she was fine. She was responding well to the treatments and I was feeling just as hopeful that the prognosis was NOT what the doctor claimed. I kept silently whispering what my mother said "the Battle is the Lords, God was in control, not man!

I was back in rhythm and successfully completed my first year of graduate school and learned we were pregnant! I was so excited, and my husband was through the moon as he was ready to start a family. Time was moving fast, baby was here and maternity leave had begun. Graduate classes remained on the weekend, internship had started and weekly transports to my mother's treatment appointments were in full swing. Life was hectic but a good hectic. It seemed things were aligned, so I thought.

My son was now two months old and I was starting summer session of classes. It was a challenging week. My mother had three treatment appointments that week. My son had well child checks, and I had a meeting with my advisor. I was feeling physically and emotionally drained, not to mention my hormones were all over the map. I was getting ready to head to class that day when I yelled out, "I'm not going, I can't do this, anymore!" My mother and husband were looking at me like I was crazy. I repeated it again, "I cannot do this!" In unison they said, "Yes you can, and you will." My husband said "You got this, you'll be fine." Tears were welling up in my eyes as he walked me to the car. He opened the door and I got in as he kissed me on my forehead.

Driving towards school, with tears running down my face, I kept thinking there is no way I can finish. Halfway there, I come to a complete stop, traffic, great! Just what I needed. The last thing I wanted was to be late for this class with a professor who was NOT sympathetic to life storms! Now, I am really working myself up in the car, crying, sweating and to make matters worse, leaking milk through my shirt. In all my hysteria, I *forgot* to pump before I left! I am thinking I have to get off this highway to go back home. But, there was nowhere for me to exit off, it was gridlocked on both sides. I was in a panic, because all I could think of was my professor's stern face, as he was a stickler for time. I knew if he said something to me, I could not guarantee, that I would not unleash on him! I thought it was another confirmation for me to quit.

I finally arrived and found a seat in the back of the class. I looked a hot mess, my hair was frizzed out, I was sweating and had two big wet spots on the front of my shirt. I purposely did not make eye contact with the professor for fear of what I might say or do. I took a deep breath and got through the class. It is funny now when I look back, at that day and how I let my emotions get the best of me. In reality, I was afraid of failing. I started thinking to myself, my mother was battling Breast Cancer, getting up every day and going to her appointments and never complained. That moment gave me a deeper perspective and greater understanding of gratitude. I realized I had nothing to complain about and I should be thankful.

There were many other occasions, when I became derailed and had to get myself back on track. In life you will find yourself in situations, that seem to be unbearable, and you do not know how you are going to get through it all. Having faith in God and allowing him to direct my steps got me through that tough time and he continues to do so.

I earned my Master of Social Work degree. I was so proud of myself, despite the negative chatter, self-doubt and challenges I faced along the way. My goal became a reality. I overcame the fear of losing my mother and quitting school. Life has its challenges, and you undoubtedly will experience them at some point. No matter what you go through, you are stronger than what you think and can get through. I am living proof. No matter how many times I wanted to throw in the towel, I persevered. Know that you have the power and control to persevere as well. At my graduation, she looked at me and said "Chris, the Battle was not yours, it was the Lords and he got you through."

About the Author

Crystal Williams is a Licensed Clinical Social Worker. She has 30 years of experience in the field of Child Welfare and clinical supervision. She has a passion for helping people overcome their struggles to be the best they can be. She resides in Connecticut with her husband and adult son. Crystal will be serving those in need of clinical support services in her private practice opening in the near future. Connect with Crystal on LinkedIn and Facebook.

Visionary Reflections

Tara Hall

The process of Emerging is about enjoying the new freedoms you choose to create for your life. Everyone has their own journey, yet as a result of reading these stories, it is my hope and goal that you have resonated with one of them, taken reflection and made a choice about how you will consider Emerging into your next season. I am in gratitude for having the privilege of coaching these women to share their unique stories of transformation with you. It all starts with a YES, to you and then a command to the universe to get into action if you are looking to be transformed.

As part of my transformational trainings, workshops, speaking engagements or coaching style, I assist others by bringing awareness to where they are and provide tools to assist in getting them to where they want to be. The process of removing doubt and fear is a journey, however knowing that you don't have to do it alone is what releases the blocks to moving forward. If you have a story to share, need a jumpstart in your life or would benefit from programs related to leadership and transformation, it's my pleasure to serve you, women's groups as well as organizations with my success based trainings and coaching. Visit and connect with me for products and services at:

www.tarahallinspiredsolutions.com

https://facebook.com/theinspiredsolutions/

LinkedIn.com/tarahallms

Instagram.com/tarad.hall

Made in the USA
Middletown, DE
09 February 2021